# 100
# Great Inventors

## 1 Johannes Gutenberg
[c. 1390 - c. 1468]

Regarded as the father of modern printing, Johannes Gutenberg invented movable-type printing for letters and symbols. Although not much is known about his life, it is believed that Gutenberg entered into a partnership with a German businessman, Johann Fust, to set up a press. It is said that Gutenberg printed the Latin Bible, which is popularly called the Gutenberg Bible in his honour. His hand-operated press used a series of blocks, each bearing a single letter on its face. The invention made copying manuscripts faster and simpler.

c.1390: Born in Mainz, Germany

c.1450: Joins with Johann Fust to set up a printing press

c.1456: Completes printing the 42-line Gutenberg Bible

February 3, 1468: Dies in Mainz, Germany

Gutenberg set up a printing press in 1450

## 2 Galileo Galilei
[1564 - 1642]

Born to a musician, Galileo first studied medicine. Soon, however, he turned his attention to mathematics, and it was in this field that Galileo left his mark. He invented the telescope and made some important discoveries. He observed that the Earth's moon had an irregular surface, and that Jupiter, too, had moons (satellites). However, his strong support for the Copernican system made him unpopular with the Church; he was placed under house arrest until his death.

Galileo Galilei

February 15, 1564: Born in Pisa, Italy

1609-10: Discovers that the surface of the moon is irregular

January 7, 1610: Discovers Jupiter's satellites

1632: Writes the famous book, Dialogue Concerning the Two Chief World Systems

January 8, 1642: Dies in Arcetri, near Florence, Italy

## 3 Cornelis Jacobszoon Drebble
[1572 - 1633]

A Dutch inventor and physicist, Drebbel is credited with many inventions such as the thermostat and a clock that could rewind constantly according to changes in the atmospheric pressure and temperature. However, Drebbel is best known for building the first navigable submarine. It consisted of a wooden frame covered with waterproof leather. The oars on its sides helped move the vessel both on the surface and underwater. Air tubes with floats provided the crew with oxygen.

1572: Born in Alkmaar, The Netherlands

1598: Receives patent for his "perpetual motion clock"

1620: First submarine voyage undertaken in the Thames River, at a depth of about 5 m (15 feet)

November 7, 1633: Dies in London, England

## 4 Evangelista Torricelli
[1608 - 1647]

*Evangelista Torricelli invented the barometer*

An Italian physicist and mathematician, Torricelli invented the barometer. Following a suggestion made by Galileo, he conducted an experiment using a glass tube filled with mercury. He observed that some of the mercury did not flow out when the tube was inverted into a dish. He also noticed a vacuum above the mercury in the tube. He realised that the height of mercury changed according to the atmospheric pressure. The barometer was thus invented. The torr, a unit of pressure, is named after him.

October 15, 1608: Born in Faenza, Italy

1641: Becomes Galileo's assistant

1643: Invents the barometer

October 25, 1647: Dies in Florence, Italy

## 5 Robert Hooke
[1635 - 1703]

July 18, 1635: Born in Freshwater, Isle of Wight, England

1655: Assists Robert Boyle, the famous chemist

1660: Discovers the law of elasticity

1665: Publishes his book, Micrographia

March 3, 1703: Dies in London

Best known for the law of elasticity named after him, English physicist Hooke is also responsible for inventions like the iris diaphragm in cameras and the universal joint used in motor vehicles. He also invented the modern air pump, the hygrometer and the reflecting telescope. He made important contributions to the fields of microbiology and geology as well.

*A modern submarine*

*Robert Hooke*

*100* GREAT
**Inventors**

## 6 Bartholomew Cristofori
[1655 - 1731]

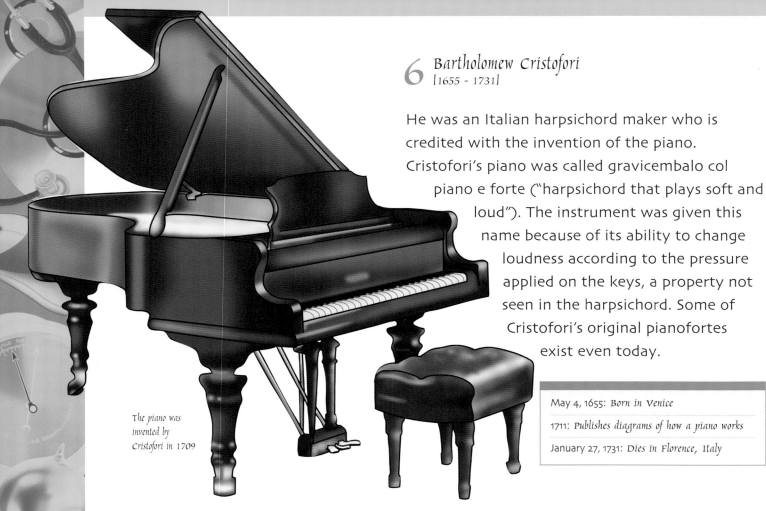

He was an Italian harpsichord maker who is credited with the invention of the piano. Cristofori's piano was called gravicembalo col piano e forte ("harpsichord that plays soft and loud"). The instrument was given this name because of its ability to change loudness according to the pressure applied on the keys, a property not seen in the harpsichord. Some of Cristofori's original pianofortes exist even today.

The piano was invented by Cristofori in 1709

May 4, 1655: Born in Venice

1711: Publishes diagrams of how a piano works

January 27, 1731: Dies in Florence, Italy

## 7 Daniel Gabriel Fahrenheit
[1686 - 1736]

May 24, 1686: Born in Gdansk, Poland

1709: Invents the alcohol thermometer

1714: Develops the mercury thermometer

September 16, 1736: Dies in Hague, Dutch Republic (now The Netherlands)

Fahrenheit was a Polish physicist who invented the alcohol thermometer. Although the first thermometers were made by Galileo, they were not reliable. Fahrenheit made the first successful thermometer using alcohol. He later developed the mercury thermometer, which gave better results. The Fahrenheit scale of temperature is named after him and is commonly used in the United States even today.

## 8 James Watt
[1736 - 1819]

January 19, 1736: Born in Greenock, Scotland

1769: Improves the Newcomen steam engine by adding a separate condenser

1775: Starts to manufacture his new engine

1782: Patents his double-acting engine in which the piston pushed and pulled

1784: Adds rods to guide the up-and-down movements of the piston

1790: Invents the pressure gauge

August 25, 1819: Dies near Birmingham, England

Watt invented the modern steam engine. Largely self-taught, Watt was working as an engineer on the Forth and Clyde Canal, when he was introduced to Thomas Newcomen's steam engine. Using a separate condenser, he reduced the loss of heat and increased the engine's efficiency. He improved it further by adding a pressure gauge and rods to guide the piston up and down. Watt also introduced the concept of horsepower. The watt, a unit of power, is named after him.

## 9 Joseph Michel Montgolfier
[1740 - 1810]

Joseph Michel and his brother Jacques Etienne invented the hot-air balloon. While watching wood chips rise over a fire, they concluded that the burning created a gas that caused any light material over it to rise. In 1783, they made the first public demonstration of their invention. The balloon rose to a height of about 1,829 m (6,000 feet) and was airborne for 10 minutes. Following several test flights, the brothers launched the first successful manned flight over Paris.

Joseph Montgolfier

August 26, 1740: *Joseph Michel is born in Annonay, France*

January 6, 1745: *Jacques Etienne is born in Annonay*

June 5, 1783: *First demonstration of the hot-air balloon*

September 19, 1783: *Sends a duck, a sheep and a rooster on a balloon flight*

November 21, 1783: *The first flight carrying people is made*

August 2, 1799: *Jacques dies on a balloon flight from Lyon to Annonay*

June 26, 1810: *Joseph Michel dies in Balaruc-les-Baines, France*

## 10 Edmund Cartwright
[1743 - 1823]

April 24, 1743: *Born in Marnharm, Nottinghamshire, England*

1785: *Patents his invention*

1789: *Obtains patent for a wool-combing machine*

October 30, 1823: *Dies in Hastings, Sussex, England*

The steam engine

This British inventor built the power loom. In the summer of 1784, after a visit to Richard Arkwright's cotton-spinning mills, Cartwright was inspired to invent a power-driven machine for weaving. The first patented machine was crude. It was strapped vertically with an overpowered shuttle and needed two men to manage it. After further improvements, the loom could be strung horizontally with decreased power. It also had devices that automatically rolled the cloth off the loom and even detected broken threads.

Edmund Cartwright

*100* GREAT
**Inventors**

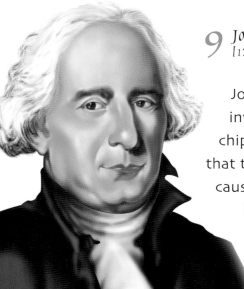

## 11 Alessandro Volta
[1745 - 1827]

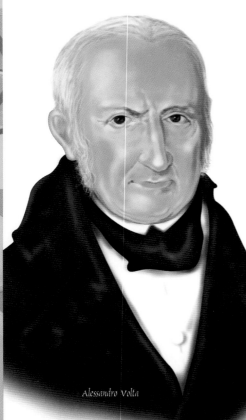

Alessandro Volta

An Italian physicist, Alessandro Volta formulated a practical method to generate continuous electric current by inventing the electric battery. He built the voltaic pile, in an attempt to disprove Luigi Galvani's theory that animal tissues contained electricity. Volta held that electricity was produced by the contact of different metals in a moist environment and that it did not require animal tissue. In 1800, he publicly demonstrated the first electric battery. In 1881, the volt, a unit of electricity, was named in his honour.

February 18, 1745: Born in Como, Lombardy, Italy

1775: Invents the electrophorus to generate static electricity

1800: Demonstrates the battery's ability to generate continuous electricity

March 5, 1827: Dies in Como, Lombardy, Italy

## 12 Nicolas Conte
[1755 - 1805]

A self-taught chemist and inventor, Nicolas-Jacques Conte was initially a painter. In 1794, there was a shortage of English graphite due to the Anglo-French war. The Committee for Public Well-Being asked Conte to produce a pencil with raw materials available in France. He did so by mixing graphite with clay. He also realised that by varying the amount of clay and graphite, it was possible to make the pencil harder or dryer. Conte's method is still used in the wood-cased pencil industry.

August 4, 1755: Born in Aunou-sur-Orne, near Sees, France

1794: Invents the modern graphite pencil

January 1795: Obtains a French patent and starts production of the Conte pencil

December 6, 1805: Dies in Paris, France

Louis-Sebastien Lenormand coined the word "parachute"

## 13 Louis-Sebastien Lenormand
[1757 - 1839]

1757: Born in France

1783: Demonstrates the principle of the parachute

1839: Dies in France

Widely regarded as the first person to jump using a parachute, there is very little information about Louis-Sebastien Lenormand. Although the Chinese are believed to have invented the parachute, Lenormand is credited with demonstrating the principle and also with the coining of the word "parachute". In 1783, he made a safe jump from a tower, using a parachute of 4.3-m (14-foot) diameter.

## 14 Robert Fulton
### [1765 - 1815]

November 14, 1765: Born in Lancaster County, Pennsylvania, U.S.

1800: Builds a submarine, the "Nautilus"

August 7, 1807: Fulton's steamboat "Clermont" is launched

1812: Builds the first steam warship

February 24, 1815: Dies in New York City

He was an American inventor who built the first commercially successful steamboat. Fulton showed an interest in engineering at a very young age. His first works included a system of inland waterways and various models of submarines and torpedoes. In 1801, American leader Robert R. Livingston asked him to build a steamboat. In 1807, Fulton's "Clermont" made the 240-km (150-mile) journey between New York City and Albany in 32 hours, one-third of the usual sailing time!

Robert Fulton

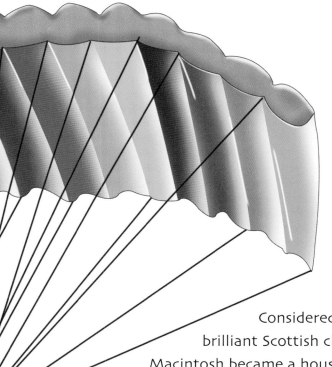

Charles Macintosh invented the first waterproof garment

## 15 Charles Macintosh
### [1766 - 1843]

Considered one of the most brilliant Scottish chemists of all times, Macintosh became a household name with his invention of the raincoat. While trying to find uses for the waste products at gasworks, Macintosh observed that naphtha obtained from coal tar could dissolve natural rubber. Encouraged by this discovery, he used the dissolved rubber to join two pieces of cloth together to produce the first waterproof garment! The material was introduced in 1824 as "Mackintosh".

December 29, 1766: Born in Glasgow, Scotland

1823: Invents the raincoat and obtains a patent for it

1834: Starts his own factory of waterproof garments

July 25, 1843: Dies near Glasgow, Scotland

## 16 Humphry Davy
[1778 - 1829]

Sir Humphry Davy established his reputation as a brilliant scientist early in his life. Though he made many valuable discoveries, his greatest contribution was the invention of the miner's safety lamp (also called Davy lamp). In 1815, Davy learnt about the dangers of the methane gas that filled the mines. The candles used by miners to light their way could spark off a fire, putting their lives in danger. So Davy replaced the candles with a flameless lamp, thus increasing safety in the mines.

| |
|---|
| December 17, 1778: Born in Penzance, Cornwall, England |
| 1799: Discovers that nitrous oxide (laughing gas) has a numbing power, ideal for use during surgery |
| 1812: Attains knighthood |
| 1815: Invents the miner's safety lamp |
| May 29, 1829: Dies in Geneva, Switzerland |

## 17 Rene Laennec
[1781 - 1826]

Rene-Theophile-Hyacinthe Laennec was the French doctor who invented the stethoscope. One day, while examining a patient, Laennec rolled up sheets of paper and placed them on his patient's chest. He was thrilled to discover that not only could he hear the sounds of the lungs and heart through the roll, but they were louder and clearer. Laennec then created the first stethoscope from a hollow piece of wood. The instrument had a hole in one end and a cone in the other.

| |
|---|
| February 17, 1781: Born in Quimper, Brittany, France |
| 1816: Invents the stethoscope |
| August 13, 1826: Dies in Kerlouanec |

The modern stethoscope

## 18 William Sturgeon
[1783 - 1850]

Son of a shoemaker, Sturgeon received very little formal education. Not wanting to become a cobbler, he ran away from home to join the army. Due to his scientific skills, he was soon made a lecturer in the Royal Military College at Addiscombe, Surrey. In 1825 he demonstrated his first electromagnet. The seven-ounce magnet could support nearly 4 kg (9 pounds) of iron when current was passed through it. His electromagnet led to the invention of the telegraph and the electric motor.

| |
|---|
| May 22, 1783: Born in Whittington, Lancashire, England |
| 1825: Invents the first electromagnet capable of supporting more than its own weight |
| 1832: Builds an electric motor and also invents the commutator used in it |
| 1836: Invents the first suspended coil galvanometer to measure current |
| December 4, 1850: Dies in Prestwich, Lancashire |

The first electromagnet was a horseshoe-shaped piece of iron that wrapped with a loosely wound coil of several turns

## 19 Samuel Morse
[1791 - 1872]

Samuel Finley Breese Morse initially chose painting as a career. However, in 1832, while travelling on the ship Sully, Morse learnt about the electromagnet. He immediately thought of making an electric telegraph. Unaware that such attempts were being made elsewhere in the world, he pursued his experiments with enthusiasm. He developed a system of using dots and dashes that became popular as the Morse Code. Upon the completion of the first American telegraph line in 1844, between Baltimore and Washington, he sent the message, "What hath God wrought!"

April 27, 1791: Born in Charlestown, Massachusetts, U.S.

1832-35: Starts work on his electric telegraph

1838: Develops the Morse code

1844: Sends the first telegraphic message

April 2, 1872: Dies in New York, U.S.

Telegraph machine

*Michael Faraday apart from inventing the electric motor also built the first generator and transformer*

## 20 Michael Faraday
[1791 - 1867]

English physicist and chemist Michael Faraday was born into a humble family. As a boy, he worked with a bookbinder, during which time he developed an interest in science. This eventually led him to become an assistant to Sir Humphry Davy, under whom he learned chemistry. However, Faraday's major contributions were to be in the fields of electricity and magnetism. He invented the dynamo and the electric motor. His observations also laid the foundations for modern electromagnetic technology.

September 22, 1791: Born in Newington, Surrey, England

1812: Becomes an assistant to Sir Humphry Davy

1821: Invents the electric motor

August 25, 1867: Dies in Hampton Court, England

## 21 Charles Babbage
[1791 - 1871]

Known as the father of computing, Charles Babbage is said to be the inventor of the first automatic digital computing machine. In an attempt to develop machines capable of complex mathematical calculations, he developed plans for the Analytical Engine. The Analytical Engine was designed to perform all kinds of arithmetical operations and was to contain a memory unit to store the numbers, along with all the other basic elements of a computer. Considered a forerunner of the modern computer, the project was, however, never completed.

December 26, 1791: Born in London

1812: Starts work on mathematical calculators

c.1821: Presents a model of the first Difference Engine, but fails to complete it

c.1833: Starts work on the Analytical Engine

October 18, 1871: Dies in London

1991: British scientists build a functional Difference Engine based on the original plans of Babbage, thus proving him correct

## 22 Mary Kies
[19th Century]

Mary Kies

May 5, 1809: Receives patent

1836: Patent file is destroyed in the great Patent Office fire

In the early 19th century, women in the United States could not patent their inventions despite a law allowing them to do so. This was mainly because in many states women could not legally own property independently. Finally, a hat-maker from Connecticut, Mary Dixon Kies, broke this pattern. She became the first woman to receive a U.S. patent, having invented a process for weaving straw with silk or thread.

## 23 Charles Wheatstone
[1802-1875]

February 6, 1802: Born in Gloucester, England

June 19, 1829: Patents the concertina

1837: Patents his electric telegraph

1841: Obtains a patent for the type-printing telegraph, the first apparatus that printed telegrams in type

1868: Receives knighthood

October 19, 1875: Dies in Paris

He was a British physicist with many innovations to his credit. However, his most famous invention is the concertina, a wind instrument with keys. Born to a musician, Wheatstone's interest in musical instruments was only natural.

He created an instrument consisting of 24 buttons (keys), metal reeds and bellows, providing wind power when operated by hand. Wheatstone also invented an early form of the microphone and made several improvements to the telegraph.

Charles Wheatstone

Charles Babbage

## 24 Louis Braille
[1809 - 1852]

January 4, 1809: Born in Coupvray, near Paris

1819: Joins the Royal Institute for Blind Youth

1824: Develops the Braille system of printing and writing

1829: Prints the first Braille book

January 6, 1852: Dies in Paris

He was a French educator who developed the Braille system of printing and writing for the blind.

Braille himself was blinded in an accident when he was three years old. While studying at the Royal Institute for Blind Youth, in Paris, he met a former soldier named Charles Barbier. Through him, Braille learnt about "night writing", a code used by French soldiers, made up of a series of 12 dots. Braille simplified it by reducing the number of dots to six. Later, in 1837, he also added symbols for math and music in the script.

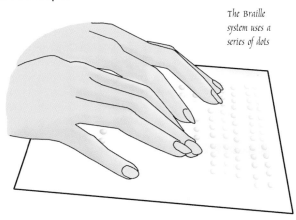

The Braille system uses a series of dots

## 25 Cyrus Hall McCormick
[1809 - 1884]

February 15, 1809: Born in Rockbridge County, Virginia, U.S.

July 1831: Develops the mechanical reaper

1834: Patents the reaper

1855: Receives the Grand Medal of Honour at a Paris exposition

May 13, 1884: Dies in Chicago, Illinois, U.S.

1902: The International Harvester Company is founded

McCormick drew his passion for invention from his father, a Virginian farmer who had patented several farming equipments. The talented son developed a mechanical reaper that combined all the steps of harvesting. After obtaining a patent for his invention, McCormick started to manufacture and sell the machine himself. Finally in 1847, he set up a factory in Chicago to mass-produce the reaper.

*100* GREAT
**Inventors**

## 26 Elisha Greaves Otis
[1811 - 1861]

Even though it is commonly believed that Otis invented the elevator, he had in fact invented the elevator brakes! However, Otis was not to know that his seemingly simple invention would make skyscrapers a reality. His safety device constituted of a steel spring catch that held the elevator even if the rope broke. At his first demonstration of this device, he had the rope cut while he was halfway up in an elevator. The platform did not fall, making his brakes a roaring success.

August 3, 1811: Born in Halifax, Vermont, U.S.

1852: Invents elevator brakes

1853: Sets up his own manufacturing unit

1854: Demonstrates his safety device at the American Institute Fair at the Crystal Palace, New York City

March 23, 1857: Installs world's first passenger safety elevator in the E.V. Haughwout and Company departmental store in New York

April 8, 1861: Dies in Yonkers, New York, U.S.

*Elisha Greaves Otis*

*Samuel Colt invented the Colt revolver*

## 27 Samuel Colt
[1814 - 1862]

July 19, 1814: Born in Hartford, Connecticut, U.S.

1830: Leaves for India by sea

1835: Patents the revolver in England and France

1836: Patents the revolver in the U.S. and establishes the Patent Arms Manufacturing Company in Paterson, New Jersey

1842: Forced to shut his factory due to poor sales

1843: Invents the first remote-controlled explosive device

1847: Resumes manufacturing guns; introduces the six-shot, .44-calibre Walker revolver

January 10, 1862: Dies in Hartford

Famous for inventing the Colt revolver, the American firearms manufacturer hit on the idea during a voyage to India. Inspired by the wheel of the ship he was on, Colt carved a wooden model of a handgun with a revolving chamber. He then spent years improving it, before first patenting the working model in 1835. He set up a company that manufactured firearms, including the famous Colt .45. His revolvers were widely used in the Mexican War and the American Civil War.

## 28 Thomas Adams
[1818 - 1905]

The modern chewing gum came about rather accidentally. The famous Mexican general Antonio Lopez de Santa Anna had asked Adams to make rubber from chicle (the milky latex of the sapodilla tree). After an unsuccessful first attempt, Adams suddenly remembered that Mexicans chewed the chicle latex. Inspired by this, he sweetened the latex and sold it as chewing gum!

1818: Born in Staten Island, New York City

1869: Creates chicle-based chewing gum

1871: Patents the first machine for manufacturing gum

1872: Creates the famous Black Jack chewing gum

1888: The Tutti-Frutti chewing gum becomes the first gum to be sold in a vending machine

1905: Dies

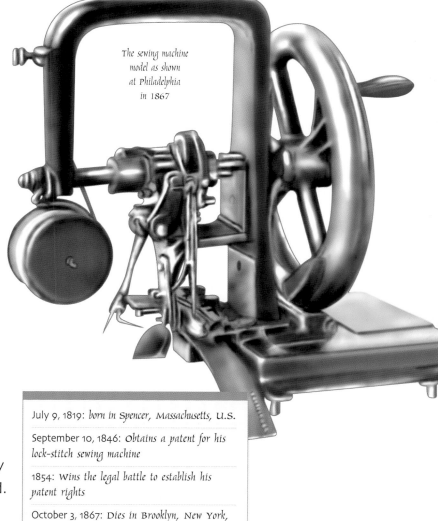

Christopher Sholes helped developed the typewriter

## 29 Christopher Latham Sholes
[1819 - 1890]

The first practical typewriter was developed by American inventor Christopher Latham Sholes. He was experimenting with a page-numbering machine, when the idea of a letter-printing machine was born. In 1868, Sholes – along with Carlos Glidden and Samuel W. Soule – obtained a patent for the typewriter. However, the keys, which were alphabetically arranged, used to get jammed when struck at a rapid pace. Sholes suggested separating the letters that most commonly appeared together, so the speed could be reduced. His new keyboard (called QWERTY, after the re-ordered keys in the uppermost row) is still in use.

February 14, 1819: *Born near Mooresburg, Pennsylvania, U.S.*

1867: *Develops the typewriter*

1873: *Sells his patent rights to the Remington Arms Company*

1874: *The Remington company starts manufacture of the "Remington typewriter"*

February 17, 1890: *Dies in Milwaukee, U.S.*

The sewing machine model as shown at Philadelphia in 1867

## 30 Elias Howe
[1819 - 1867]

Howe first came up with the idea of his sewing machine while working at a textile mill. A needle with an eye at its sharp point pushes the thread through the fabric to form a loop. The loop is caught by a mechanism below the fabric. The next loop from the needle is then pulled through the first loop to form a lock stitch. The speed of the machine completely changed the way cloths were manufactured. However, despite having patented his machine, Howe had to fight a legal battle with co-inventors Issac Singer and Allen Wilson, before he was given due credit.

July 9, 1819: *born in Spencer, Massachusetts, U.S.*

September 10, 1846: *Obtains a patent for his lock-stitch sewing machine*

1854: *Wins the legal battle to establish his patent rights*

October 3, 1867: *Dies in Brooklyn, New York, U.S.*

100 GREAT
# Inventors

## 31 Levi Strauss
[1829 - 1902]

Levi Strauss moved to San Francisco to set up a dry-goods business. His customers included a tailor named Jacob Davis. Davis had invented a unique method to make sturdy work pants, by putting metal rivets on the pocket corners and at the base of the zipper. Not having enough money for a patent application, Davis approached Levi. Together, they patented this innovation that marked the birth of jeans. It is believed that their pants were made from a material from France called "serge de Nimes", now famous as denim!

*The old name for "jeans" was "waist overalls"*

**February 26, 1829:** Born in Buttenheim, Bavaria

**1847:** Goes to New York, U.S.

**1853:** Becomes an American citizen; sets up business in San Francisco

**May 20, 1873:** Receives patent for an "improvement in fastening pocket openings"; starts making copper-riveted "waist overalls" (old name for "jeans")

**September 27, 1902:** Dies in San Francisco, U.S.

## 32 George Pullman
[1831 - 1897]

**March 3, 1831:** Born in Brocton, New York, U.S.

**1867:** Establishes the Pullman Palace Car Company to build sleeping cars

**1868:** Introduces dining cars

**1880:** Establishes the town of Pullman near Chicago

**October 19, 1897:** Dies in Pullman Town, Chicago

George Mortimer Pullman was an American inventor who designed the sleeping car for trains. The first Pullman sleeping car, the "Pioneer", was invented with Ben Field and introduced in 1865. It included folding upper berths, a feature still in use. Pullman's car received nationwide publicity when it carried the departed president Abraham Lincoln's body across the country.

*George Pullman's sleeping cars*

## 33 Nikolaus August Otto
[1832 - 1891]

**June 10, 1832:** Born in Holzhausen, Nassau, Germany

**1861:** Builds his first gasoline engine

**January 26, 1891:** Dies in Cologne, Germany

He was a German engineer who developed the four-stroke internal-combustion engine in 1876. This engine's piston moves up and down four times, giving the engine its name. The piston movements draw in fuel and air and compress the mixture in a cylinder, thereby causing an internal explosion. Because of its dependability, efficiency and quietness, over 30,000 Otto cycle engines were built within a decade.

## 34 Alfred Nobel
[1833 - 1896]

Alfred Bernhard Nobel is famous for inventing dynamite. Aware of the dangers of liquid nitroglycerine (an explosive), Nobel devised a method of solidifying the substance. He patented what he called "dynamite" in 1867. Besides explosives, Nobel made several chemical inventions and held 355 patents in various countries. He left a huge part of his wealth to establish the Nobel Prize, reflecting his keen interest in the sciences, literature and world peace.

*Nobel invented dynamite in 1866*

*Alfred Nobel*

October 21, 1833: Born in Stockholm, Sweden

1863: Receives patent for a detonator that used electrical shock, rather than heat, to cause explosion

1866: Invents dynamite

1867: Granted patent for dynamite

1875: Invents blasting gelatine

1887: Obtains patent for a smokeless blasting powder, "ballistite"

November 27, 1895: Signs his final will at the Swedish-Norwegian club in Paris, leaving his wealth to constitute the Nobel Prize

December 10, 1896: Dies in San Remo, Italy

## 35 Gottlieb Wilhelm Daimler
[1834 - 1900]

Daimler was one of the pioneers of the automotive industry. Attempting to improve the Otto cycle engine, Daimler and his friend Wilhelm Maybach came up with an improved version of the engine. It was lightweight, fast and more efficient. Later, the twosome created what is believed to be the world's first motorcycle, by attaching the engine to a bicycle! They also developed the first four-wheeled motor car by adapting an engine to a horse-carriage. It is said that Daimler – a person who revolutionised the car industry – did not like to drive!

*The first motorcycle was a bicycle fitted with an engine!*

March 17, 1834: Born in Schorndorf, Wurttemberg, Germany

1872: Works as technical director at Nikolaus Otto's company

1882: Starts his own company with Wilhelm Maybach

1885: Patents the Daimler engine and invents the motorcycle

1886: Creates the first four-wheeled motor car

1890: Establishes the Daimler Company in Cannstatt

1899: Designs the first Mercedes car, named after his partner Emil Jellinek's daughter

March 6, 1900: Dies in Cannstatt, near Stuttgart

*100* GREAT
**Inventors**

## 36 Lewis Edson Waterman
[1837 - 1901]

1837: Born in Decatur, Otsego County, New York

1899: Opens a pen factory at Montreal

1901: Dies, leaving the business to his nephew, Frank D. Waterman

Waterman was an insurance agent who invented the capillary feed in fountain pens. In 1883, he had bought a new fountain pen on the occasion of the signing of a big contract. However, just as the client was about to sign, the ink leaked on to the document! Waterman lost the contract to his competitor. Unhappy with the turn of events, he began making his own fountain pens. He used the capillary principle, by which the ink flow was controlled and made steady. He called his pen "the Regular" and patented it in 1884.

## 37 John Dunlop
[1840 - 1921]

February 5, 1840: Born in Dreghorn, North Ayrshire, Scotland

1867: Moves to Belfast, Ireland

1888: Patents the "pneumatic" tyre

October 24, 1921: Dies in Dublin, Ireland

Scottish veterinarian John Boyd Dunlop developed the famous pneumatic (air-filled) tyre quite by accident. One day, while watching his son ride a tricycle, Dunlop noticed the boy's discomfort whenever he rode over stones. He realised that this was because of the tyres. So he wrapped the wheels in thin rubber sheets and glued them together. He then inflated them for a cushioning effect, thus making the first pneumatic tyre. Ten years later, his tyre had almost wiped out the solid tyres.

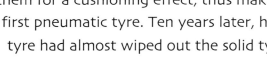

## 38 James Dewar
[1842 - 1923]

A double walled vacuum flask

September 20, 1842: Born in Kincardine-on-Forth, Scotland

1889: Co-invents cordite, an explosive used extensively in World War I

1892: Invents the vacuum flask

1899: Succeeds in liquefying hydrogen

1904: Receives knighthood

1921: Measures solar radiation using instruments cooled with liquid oxygen

March 27, 1923: Dies in London

He was a British chemist and inventor, best known for creating the thermos flask. While studying gases at low temperature, Sir Dewar built a double-walled vacuum flask made of glass. Later, he realized that using metal would make it stronger. However, the surface of the metal absorbed the gas, making the vacuum ineffective. In 1905, he found that placing a piece of charcoal into the flask and cooling it, solved the problem. He also painted the inside of the flask with silver to reduce radiation.

## 39 Karl Friedrich Benz
### [1844 - 1929]

He is considered to be one of the inventors of the gasoline-powered motor car. In 1885, Karl Benz built his first three-wheeler with a four-stroke engine. However, it drew little public interest initially. So, his wife Bertha Benz embarked on a secret trip from Mannheim to Pforzheim – the first long-distance trip in motor-car history! When news about Bertha's adventurous journey spread, demand for the car started pouring in.

Inflated tyres are extensively used today

November 25, 1844: Born in Karlsruhe, Baden, Germany

1872: Marries Bertha Ringer

1879: Invents a two-stroke engine

1883: Establishes the Benz & Co. company with Max Rose and Friedrich Wilhelm Esslinger, in Mannheim

1886: Introduces the "Benz Patent Motor Car"

1903: Resigns from the company

1926: Benz & Co. merges with Daimler-Motoren-Gesellschaft (DMG)

April 4, 1929: Dies in Ladenburg, near Mannheim, Germany

Karl Friedrich Benz

## 40 George Westinghouse
### [1846 - 1914]

One of the most famous American inventors of the 19th century, Westinghouse made invaluable contributions to the railway industry. His inventions included a rotary steam engine and a switch that enabled a train to pass over intersecting rails at junctions. However, he is best remembered for developing the first successful brake system that used compressed air. This system proved more effective than the existing manual brake in preventing accidents.

George Westinghouse

October 6, 1846: Born in Central Bridge, New York, U.S.

1865: Receives patent for the rotary steam engine

1868: Invents the air brake system; obtains patent in 1869

March 12, 1914: Dies in New York City

*100* GREAT
**Inventors**

## 41 Thomas Alva Edison
[1847 - 1931]

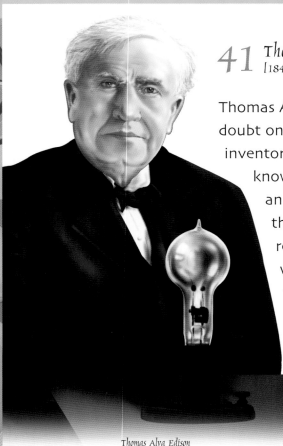

Thomas Alva Edison is without doubt one of the greatest inventors the world has ever known. Edison's genius as an inventor is clear from the fact that he held a record 1,093 patents, of which almost 400 were for electric light and power! Among his most famous inventions were the carbon-button transmitter (1877), the phonograph (1877), the incandescent light bulb (1879) and the motion-picture camera (1891). Edison also established the first-ever industrial-research laboratory.

Thomas Alva Edison

| |
|---|
| February 11, 1847: Born in Milan, Ohio, U.S. |
| 1862-68: Works as a telegrapher |
| 1868: Patents the electrical vote recorder |
| 1871: Helps Sholes to make the first working model of the typewriter |
| 1877: Invents the carbon-button transmitter that is still used in telephones and microphones |
| 1914: Invents the Telescribe, thus making it possible to record both sides of a telephone conversation for the first time |
| October 18, 1931: Dies in New Jersey, U.S. |

## 42 Alexander Graham Bell
[1847 - 1922]

By inventing the telephone, Bell revolutionised communication as we see it today. His invention gave the words "a small world" a whole new meaning. Bell had been toying with the idea of transmitting voice from a very young age. While working on improving the telegraph, he came up with the idea of a telephone. He started to work tirelessly with his assistant Thomas Watson. Finally, on March 10, 1876, Bell transmitted the first complete sentence. He also invented the photophone and the graphophone.

| |
|---|
| March 3, 1847: Born in Edinburgh, Scotland |
| 1871: Moves to the United States |
| 1872: Establishes a school for training teachers of the deaf, in Boston, Massachusetts |
| 1882: Becomes a U.S. citizen |
| 1876: Invents and patents the telephone |
| 1877: Co-founds the Bell Telephone Company |
| August 2, 1922: Dies in Beinn Bhreagh, Cape Breton Island, Nova Scotia, Canada |

## 43 Walter Hunt
[1796 - 1859]

Though pins had been in use years before Hunt's safety pin, they did not have a protective clasp. Hunt's safety pin not only had a clasp, but also a spring that held the two ends together. Apparently, Hunt was twisting a piece of wire and trying to think of a way to settle a $15 debt, when he accidentally invented the safety pin. Upon realising that he had created something of great use, Hunt patented what he called the "dress pin". However, he sold the rights for a paltry sum of $400 to pay off his debt.

## 44 Karl Braun
### [1850 - 1918]

Karl Ferdinand Braun was a German inventor who won the 1909 Nobel Prize in Physics for his contributions to wireless telegraphy. However, he is best known as the inventor of the cathode-ray tube, or "Braun tube". Braun developed his idea from the premise that when two electrodes are subjected to high voltage, the electrons from the cathode (negative electrode) travel to the anode (positive electrode). He built what he called the "cathode-ray indicator tube", which is an integral part of the modern television.

June 6, 1850: *Born in Fulda, Hesse-Kassel (now in Germany)*

1897: *Invents the cathode-ray tube, but does not patent his invention*

1898: *Starts work on improving wireless telegraphy*

1909: *Shares the Nobel Prize in Physics with Guglielmo Marconi*

April 20, 1918: *Dies in Brooklyn, New York*

*Karl Braun*

*An early wall-hung telephone*

*The safety pin was first created by Walter Hunt*

July 29, 1796: *Born in Martinsburg, New York*

c. 1834: *Invents the modern sewing machine before Elias Howe, but does not patent it, fearing it would cause unemployment*

April 10, 1849: *Patents the safety pin*

June 8, 1859: *Dies*

## 45 John Milne
### [1850 - 1913]

Widely accepted as the father of seismology, John Milne invented the seismograph, an instrument used to study earthquakes. A geologist and mining engineer, Milne became interested in the study of earthquakes while in Japan. He set up the world's first seismological society and conducted extensive research on Japanese earthquakes. During this time, he also invented the seismograph.

December 30, 1850: *Born in Liverpool, England*

1880: *Invents the horizontal pendulum seismograph; establishes the Seismological Society of Japan with colleagues Sir James Alfred Ewing and Thomas Gray*

February 17, 1895: *A fire destroys his home, observatory and library*

1895: *Returns to England; settles on the Isle of Wight and promotes establishment of earthquake observatories across the world*

July 30, 1913: *Dies in Shide, Isle of Wight*

## 46 Emil Berliner
[1851 - 1929]

Emil Berliner

Emil (also spelt Emile) Berliner improved Bell's telephone with a "loose-contact" transmitter. It was a type of microphone that increased the volume of the transmitted voice. A still more significant invention by Emil was the disc record gramophone.

Unlike Edison's cylinder gramophone, Berliner's used a flat disc. This enabled inexpensive, mass production of gramophones. Emil was also behind the famous trademark of a dog listening to "his master's voice" on the gramophone. It was originally a painting by Francis Barraud.

| |
|---|
| May 20, 1851: Born in Hannover, Hanover, Germany |
| 1870: Moves to the United States |
| 1876: Invents the "loose-contact" transmitter |
| 1887: Patents his gramophone |
| 1893: Forms the United States Gramophone Company of Washington, D.C. |
| 1895: Establishes the Berliner Gramophone Company of Philadelphia |
| 1898: Opens the Berliner Gramophone Company of London |
| August 3, 1929: Dies in Washington, D.C., U.S. |

## 47 George Eastman
[1854 - 1932]

An American inventor, George Eastman developed the dry roll film and the hand-held camera. After working briefly for a bank, Eastman turned his attention to making photographic film rolls. Having made the first film roll, Eastman invented a small hand-held camera he named Kodak. The success of his inventions spurred him on to establish the Eastman Kodak Company, the first of its kind to mass-produce photography equipment.

| |
|---|
| July 12, 1854: Born in Waterville, New York |
| 1880: Patents a dry-plate formula and a machine for making it |
| 1885: Introduces the first transparent photographic film |
| 1888: Introduces the Kodak camera |
| 1889: Invents the first transparent roll film, leading to Edison's invention of the motion-picture camera |
| March 14, 1932: Dies in Rochester, New York |

## 48 King Camp Gillette
[1855 - 1932]

*Gillette played an important role in making razors popular*

King Camp Gillette is incorrectly known as the inventor of the safety razor. However, his disposable steel blade certainly played a vital role in the razor's popularity. Gillette was forced to work at a young age, after his family lost everything in the Great Chicago Fire of 1871. As a travelling salesman, Gillette came up with an idea of an inexpensive safety razor blade that could be replaced easily.

| |
|---|
| January 5, 1855: Born in Wisconsin, U.S. |
| September 28, 1901: Establishes the American Safety Razor company |
| 1903: First razors are produced; about 51 razors and 168 blades are sold |
| 1904: Sells some 90,884 razors and 123,648 blades |
| July 9, 1932: Dies in Los Angeles, California, U.S. |

## 49 Nikola Tesla
### [1856 - 1943]

Serbian by birth, Tesla arrived in the United States in 1884. The very next year, he sold the patent rights to his system of alternating-current dynamos and transformers to George Westinghouse. Tesla's electric transformers revolutionised the power industry by helping the production of alternating current. Westinghouse used the system to light the World's Columbian Exposition at Chicago in 1893. As a result, Tesla won the contract to install a power station at Niagara Falls. However, his biggest contribution was in the form of the induction coil (named Tesla coil in his honour), which continues to be used in radios and televisions.

| |
|---|
| July 9/10, 1856: *Born in Smiljan, Croatia* |
| 1884: *Arrives in New York and briefly works under Thomas Alva Edison* |
| 1891: *Invents the Tesla coil* |
| 1899-1900: *Proves that earth can be used as a conductor* |
| January 7, 1943: *Dies in New York City* |

## 50 Rudolf Diesel
### [1858 - 1913]

Famous for developing a pressure-ignited heat engine named after him, Diesel's invention was inspired by a cigarette lighter. He noted with fascination that the piston in a lighter compressed the air in a glass tube, causing the tinder in it to glow. He immediately began his 13-year-long labour to create and perfect an economical – yet highly efficient – alternative to the steam engine. His engine soon became popular and was used extensively in ships, electric power plants, oil drills and, eventually, automobiles.

*George Eastman was a pioneer in the photography industry. He invented the first hand held camera.*

*Rudolf Diesel*

| |
|---|
| March 18, 1858: *Born in Paris, France* |
| 1898: *Patents the diesel engine* |
| September 29, 1913: *Dies by drowning in the English Channel* |

## 51 George Ferris
[1859 - 1896]

George Washington Gale Ferris, Jr., invented the Ferris wheel. A bridge builder by profession, Ferris built the wheel for the 1893 World's Columbian Fair, to rival the Eiffel Tower of the 1889 Paris World's Fair. Ferris' wheel was about 76 m (250 feet) in diameter and had 36 cars. Each car could carry around 40 passengers. A huge success then, the Ferris wheel continues to be a major part of the American carnivals.

*George Ferris*

February 14, 1859: *Born in Galesburg, Illinois, U.S.*

June 21, 1893: *The Ferris wheel is inaugurated*

November 22, 1896: *Dies in Pittsburgh, U.S.*

## 52 Schuyler Wheeler
[1860 - 1923]

1882: *Develops the electric fan*

Dr. Schuyler Skaats Wheeler invented the electric fan. The story goes that the idea occurred to him while he watched a ferry on the Hudson River. He observed that the propeller of the ferry created waves on the water. Realising that the same mechanism can produce cool air, Wheeler created the first electric fan using two metal blades. His model consisted of a propeller attached to a shaft that was operated by an electric motor.

*Schuyler Wheeler's electric fan had only two blades*

## 53 Jesse Wilford Reno
[1861 - unknown]

Inventor of the escalator, Jesse Reno thought of the idea at the young age of 16. While in Georgia, Reno first gave shape to his idea and obtained a patent for his "endless conveyor". Reno first installed his moving stairway as an amusement ride in Coney Island, Brooklyn. The popularity of the ride brought Reno's invention into the limelight and soon he was swamped by orders from all over the world. Reno's escalator had stationary handrails that were later replaced with moving handrails.

1861: *Born in Fort Leavenworth, Kansas, U.S.*

1891: *Invents the escalator*

March 15, 1892: *Patents his invention*

1895: *Installs the escalator in Coney Island*

1902: *Establishes the Reno Electric Stairways and Conveyors Limited in London*

1911: *Sells his patent rights to Otis Elevator Company*

## 54 Henry Ford
[1863 - 1947]

His biggest contribution to the automotive industry was the assembly-line production method. In this system, the workers stood in one place and added a part to each vehicle as it moved past them. This made the manufacturing and assembling process much easier and also increased the number of cars produced. Not only did it mark the beginning of a revolution in the car industry, it also made Ford's company a giant in its field.

July 30, 1863: *Born in Wayne county, Michigan, U.S.*

1896: *Constructs a four-wheeled car*

1903: *Establishes the Ford Motor Company*

1908: *Introduces the famous Model T car*

1913: *Introduces the assembly-line production method*

April 7, 1947: *Dies in Dearborn, Michigan, U.S.*

*The Model-T was the first car to be made using the assembly line*

## 55 Leo Baekeland
[1863 - 1944]

Baekeland's invention of bakelite, a plastic that cannot be melted by heat, helped establish the plastic industry. His first invention was Velox, a photographic paper that could be developed under artificial light. He, however, sold the patent rights to George Eastman for a million dollars and set up a laboratory. Later, while attempting to make a synthetic alternative for shellac, he created bakelite. Today, bakelite is used in cars, electronics and even jewellery.

November 14, 1863: *Born in Ghent, Belgium*

1889: *Arrives in U.S.*

1893: *Invents Velox*

1899: *Sells his patent rights to George Eastman*

1909: *Invents bakelite*

1910: *Establishes the Bakelite Corporation*

February 23, 1944: *Dies in Beacon, New York*

*Leo Baekeland*

*100* GREAT
**Inventors**

## 56 Wilbur and Orville Wright
[1867 - 1912] [1871 - 1948]

| |
|---|
| April 16, 1867: Wilbur is born in Millville, Indianapolis, U.S |
| August 19, 1871: Orville is born in Dayton, Ohio, U.S. |
| 1889: Open a printing business |
| 1892: Start their bicycle business |
| December 17, 1903: Orville flies the first Wright flyer at Kitty Hawk, North Carolina; lasts 12 seconds over a distance of 36.6 m (120 feet). Wilbur's flight lasts for 59 seconds and covers 260 m (852 feet) |
| 1906: Obtain patent for their flyer |
| May 1908: The brothers carry a passenger on the plane for the first time |
| August 1908: The first public exhibition flight takes place at Le Mans in France |
| 1910: Make their first and only flight together |
| May 30, 1912: Wilbur dies of typhoid fever in Dayton, Ohio |
| January 30, 1948: Orville dies in Dayton |

December 17, 1903, is the most memorable day in the history of aviation. This was the day when Wilbur Wright and his brother Orville accomplished the first-ever powered and controlled aeroplane flight. Born into a humble family, the Wright brothers worked towards their dream by making bicycles. Inspired by the German glider Otto Lilienthal, the brothers constructed the Wright flyer. Among other ground-breaking features, the plane had the first lightweight engine and movable wing tips that helped control it.

## 57 Valdemar Poulsen
[1869 - 1942]

| |
|---|
| November 23, 1869: Born in Copenhagen, Denmark |
| 1898: Patents the telegraphone |
| 1903: Patents the Poulsen arc transmitter |
| July 1942: Dies in Copenhagen |

Poulsen took to engineering early on in his life. Working at the technical department at the Copenhagen Telephone Company, he invented the telegraphone, a forerunner of the modern tape recorder. Using his "telegrafoon", Poulsen demonstrated that it was possible to record and play back voices on a magnetised steel wire. He also invented the Poulsen arc transmitter for producing continuous radio waves, thus contributing to the development of radio broadcasting.

## 58 Guglielmo Marconi
[1874 - 1937]

| |
|---|
| April 25, 1874: Born in Bologna, Italy |
| 1896: Invents and patents a successful system of wireless telegraphy |
| 1897: Establishes the Wireless Telegraphy & Signal Company Limited in London |
| 1899: Sends signals from England to France |
| 1901: Sends signals across the Atlantic, between Cornwall and Newfoundland |
| 1909: Wins the Nobel Prize in Physics for his contributions to wireless telegraphy |
| July 20, 1937: Dies in Rome, Italy |

At the age of 21, Marconi invented the first practical system of wireless telegraphy. He continued to improve his device and succeeded in sending signals across the English Channel to France. In 1901, he proved that the wireless waves are not affected by the Earth's curvature. He did this by transmitting signals across the Atlantic Ocean covering a distance of about 3,380 km (2,100 miles).

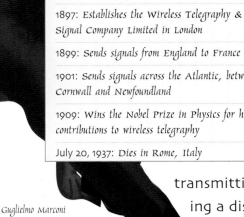

Guglielmo Marconi

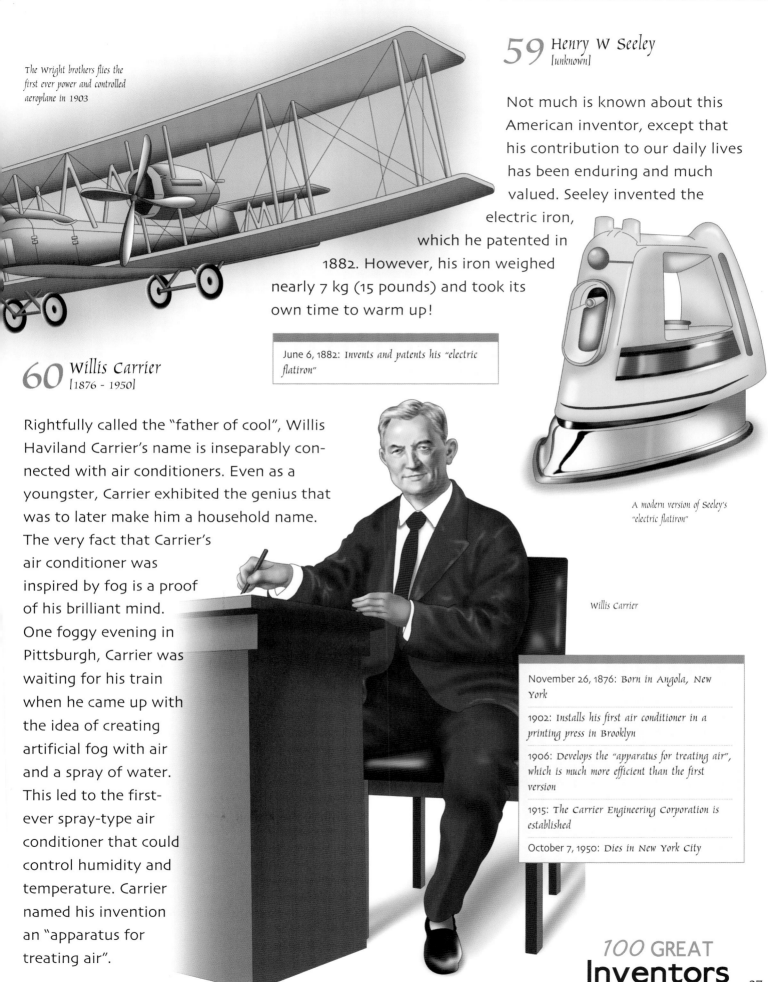

The Wright brothers flies the first ever power and controlled aeroplane in 1903

## 59 Henry W Seeley
[unknown]

Not much is known about this American inventor, except that his contribution to our daily lives has been enduring and much valued. Seeley invented the electric iron, which he patented in 1882. However, his iron weighed nearly 7 kg (15 pounds) and took its own time to warm up!

June 6, 1882: *Invents and patents his "electric flatiron"*

A modern version of Seeley's "electric flatiron"

## 60 Willis Carrier
[1876 - 1950]

Rightfully called the "father of cool", Willis Haviland Carrier's name is inseparably connected with air conditioners. Even as a youngster, Carrier exhibited the genius that was to later make him a household name. The very fact that Carrier's air conditioner was inspired by fog is a proof of his brilliant mind. One foggy evening in Pittsburgh, Carrier was waiting for his train when he came up with the idea of creating artificial fog with air and a spray of water. This led to the first-ever spray-type air conditioner that could control humidity and temperature. Carrier named his invention an "apparatus for treating air".

Willis Carrier

November 26, 1876: *Born in Angola, New York*

1902: *Installs his first air conditioner in a printing press in Brooklyn*

1906: *Develops the "apparatus for treating air", which is much more efficient than the first version*

1915: *The Carrier Engineering Corporation is established*

October 7, 1950: *Dies in New York City*

*100* GREAT
Inventors

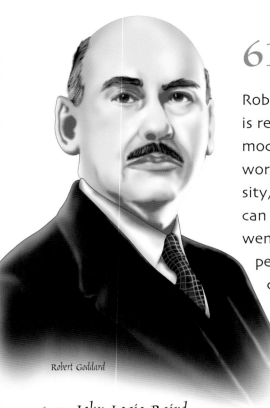
Robert Goddard

## 61 Robert Goddard
[1882 - 1945]

Robert Hutchings Goddard is regarded as the father of modern rocketry. While working at the Clark University, he proved that a rocket can work in a vacuum. He went on to become the first person to develop and successfully launch a liquid-fuelled rocket engine. Apart from this, Goddard developed rocket-fuel pumps and self-cooling rocket engines. He also patented the automatic steering apparatus for rockets.

October 5, 1882: Born in Worcester, Massachusetts, U.S.

1914: Receives a patent for his liquid-fuelled rocket

1918: Develops the "bazooka"

1919: Publishes his famous book, A Method of Reaching Extreme Altitudes

March 16, 1926: Launches the world's first liquid-fuelled rocket from a farm in Auburn, Massachusetts

August 10, 1945: Dies in Baltimore, U.S.

## 62 John Logie Baird
[1888 - 1946]

John Logie Baird earlier tried his hand at selling medicated socks and also set up jam and soap factories in Trinidad. The mixed response forced him to wind up his business and return to Britain. Baird then created a crude version of the television. The apparatus consisted of a motor on a tea chest. A biscuit tin held the projection lamp, while round pieces of cardboard served as scanning discs!

Igor Sikorsky

## 63 Igor Sikorsky
[1889-1972]

Igor Sikorsky designed the first multi-motor aeroplane as well as the modern helicopter. Forced to leave Russia after the 1917 Revolution, Sikorsky first moved to France and eventually to the United States. At Long Island, New York, he established the Sikorsky Aero Engineering Corporation. Afterwards, he designed a twin-engine amphibian aircraft and a successful model of the helicopter. Sikorsky's single-rotor design continues to be used in helicopters.

May 25, 1889: Born in Kiev, Russia

1913: Builds the first four-engine aeroplane with an enclosed cabin

1919: Goes to the U.S.

1923: Establishes his company

1931: Designs the two-engine amphibian aircraft

1939: Designs the modern helicopter

October 26, 1972: Dies in Connecticut, U.S.

## 64 Sir Robert Alexander Watson-Watt
[1892 - 1973]

He started his career as a meteorologist, using his knowledge of radio to locate thunderstorms. During this period he realised the need for a method to locate aircraft. In 1919, he patented a device that used short-wave radio waves to locate aeroplanes. He continued to improve this device and soon came up with the radar concept – sending out radio waves to aeroplanes, receiving their reflections and using the intervening time to calculate the distance. His radar system played an important role in the defeat of Germany during World War II.

John Logie Baird

> April 13, 1892: Born in Brechin, Angus, Scotland
>
> 1919: Patents his radio-location device
>
> 1940: His radars help Britain counter German air raids
>
> 1942: Receives knighthood
>
> December 5, 1973: Dies in Inverness, Inverness-shire, Scotland

> August 13, 1888: Born in Helensburgh, Dunbarton, Scotland
>
> 1924: Becomes the first to transmit a moving image
>
> 1926: Demonstrates his television to scientists from the Royal Institution, London
>
> 1927: Establishes the Baird Television Development Company
>
> 1928: Transmits images across the Atlantic to New York
>
> 1931: Achieves the first live transmission of the Epsom Derby
>
> June 14, 1946: Dies in Sussex, England

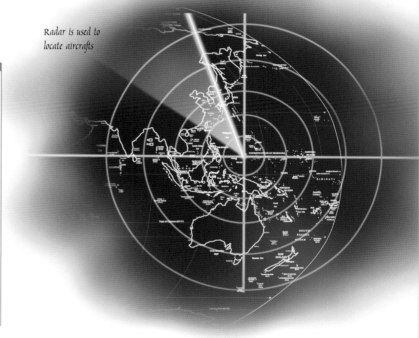
Radar is used to locate aircrafts

## 65 John Larson
[c. 1892 - c. 1983]

John Larson invented the polygraph, popularly called the lie-detector test. A police officer, Larson was fascinated by the possibility of being able to determine whether a person was telling the truth or not. Although the concept of lie detector was not alien, Larson built a unique machine that could record changes in blood pressure, pulse and respiration. His system was adopted by the police in 1924. Later, his student Leonarde Keeler replaced it with a more effective version.

> c.1892: Born in the United States
>
> 1921: Develops the polygraph test
>
> c.1983: Dies

*100* GREAT
**Inventors**

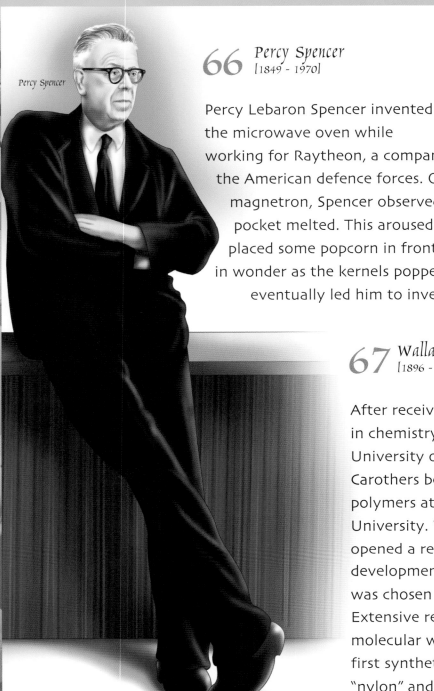

Percy Spencer

## 66 Percy Spencer
[1849 - 1970]

July 19, 1849: Born in Howland, Maine, U.S.

1945: Invents the microwave oven

September 8, 1970: Dies

Percy Lebaron Spencer invented the microwave oven while working for Raytheon, a company that produced radars for the American defence forces. One day as he stood near a magnetron, Spencer observed that the chocolate bar in his pocket melted. This aroused his curiosity. He immediately placed some popcorn in front of the magnetron and watched in wonder as the kernels popped. This simple experiment eventually led him to invent the microwave oven.

## 67 Wallace Hume Carothers
[1896 - 1937]

*Nylon is extensively used to make ropes.*

After receiving his PhD in chemistry from the University of Illinois, Carothers began research on polymers at Harvard University. When DuPont opened a research laboratory for the development of artificial material, Carothers was chosen to lead its research team. Extensive research on the compounds of high molecular weight led to the creation of the first synthetic polymer fibre, later named "nylon" and a synthetic rubber, neoprene.

## 68 Mary Anderson
[unknown - ]

1903: Thinks of the idea for the windshield wiper

1905: Obtains patent

1913: Mechanical windshield wipers become a regular feature of cars

Until 1903, car drivers had their own way of coping with the rainwater that fell on the windshields. Usually the annoyed driver would stop the car and manually wipe the windshield. Mary Anderson was to change all that by inventing the windshield wiper. The idea occurred to her when she saw drivers in New York City constantly stopping their cars to remove snow and moisture from their windshields. Anderson's wiper consisted of a lever that could be operated from inside the car. When switched on, the lever activated an arm equipped with a rubber blade.

## 69 Ernest Lawrence
[1901 - 1958]

Ernest Orlando Lawrence invented the cyclotron, a device that can cause nuclear particles to move at very high speed without the use of high voltages. These fast-moving particles can be used to strike atoms and split them. Lawrence's first model of the cyclotron was made of wire and sealing wax. Its successful demonstration not only made Lawrence famous, but also contributed to the making of the atom bomb.

August 8, 1901: Born in Canton, South Dakota, U.S.

1929: Develops the cyclotron

1939: Receives the Nobel Prize in Physics

1957: Receives the Enrico Fermi Award

August 27, 1958: Dies in Palo Alto, California

Ernest Lawrence

April 27, 1896: Born in Burlington, Iowa, U.S.

1928: Joins DuPont and starts research on artificial materials

April 1930: His assistant, Arnold M. Collins, isolates neoprene

1934: Develops nylon

April 29, 1937: Takes his own life

1939: Mass production of nylon begins

William Lear set up a company to produce small private planes

## 70 William Lear
[1902 - 1978]

An American inventor of great repute, William Lear's name is usually associated with the jet plane named after him. His most significant invention, though, was the car radio. Having developed the car radio, Lear sold it to Galvin Manufacturing Company, to be marketed under the brand name Motorola. In 1963, he established Lear Jet Incorporated to produce small private aircraft, which soon became popular with big companies. The following year, he invented the eight-track stereo that laid the foundations for the car-stereo industry.

June 26, 1902: Born in Hannibal, Missouri, U.S.

1930: Designs the car radio

1964: Develops the eight-track car stereo

May 14, 1978: Dies in Reno, Nevada, U.S.

*100* GREAT
**Inventors**

## 71 Chester Carlson
[1906 - 1968]

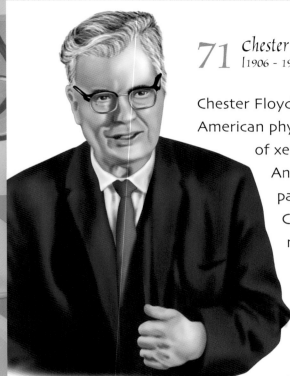
Chester Carlson

Chester Floyd Carlson was an American physicist and the inventor of xerography (photocopy). An employee at the patent department, Carlson was required to make copies of patent drawings and other documents. While most people then depended on chemical solutions to produce copies, Carlson investigated ways to obtain "dry copies". In 1938, he succeeded in producing copies using photoconduction process.

| |
|---|
| February 8, 1906: Born in Seattle, Washington, U.S. |
| 1938: Develops the photocopying process |
| 1940: Obtains patent for his invention |
| 1944: Signs an agreement with Battelle Development Corporation for further research on the process |
| 1947: Sells his rights to the Haloid Company (later renamed Xerox Corporation) |
| 1958: Xerox launches its first office copier |
| September 19, 1968: Dies in New York City |

## 72 Frank Whittle
[1907 - 1996]

While serving as a pilot with the Royal Air Force (RAF), Whittle realised the potential of developing a plane that could fly at high speed and altitude. He started working on an engine that used a "jet" of air for movement. Although the air ministry rejected the idea in the beginning, Whittle patented it and established Power Jets Limited to continue his research. After several modifications, the jet engine was finally ready to take flight on May 15, 1941.

| |
|---|
| June 1, 1907: Born in Coventry, Warwickshire, England |
| 1928: Qualifies as a pilot in the RAF |
| 1930: Patents his jet engine |
| 1936: Establishes Power Jets Limited |
| 1948: Retires from the RAF as air commodore |
| 1948: Attains knighthood; moves to the United States |
| 1976: Becomes a research professor at the U.S. Naval Academy, Maryland |
| 1986: Awarded the Order of Merit |
| August 9, 1996: Dies in Baltimore, Maryland, U.S. |

## 73 George de Mestral
[1907 - 1990]

Like many other inventions, the Velcro was also invented accidentally. Returning from his walk one day, George de Mestral found cockleburs (weeds with hooks) stuck to his clothes. Fascinated, Mestral examined one of them under a microscope and found the tiny hooks that helped the cocklebur to attach itself to cloth or fur. After eight years of experiment, Mestral developed and perfected what he named "Velcro".

| |
|---|
| June 19, 1907: Born near Lausanne, Switzerland |
| 1948: Conceives of the Velcro |
| 1955: Obtains patent for his invention |
| February 8, 1990: Dies |

## 74 John Bardeen
[1908 - 1991]

*The transistor was co-invented by John Bardeen*

American physicist and co-inventor of the transistor, John Bardeen is the only scientist to have won the Nobel Prize in Physics twice. After World War II, Bardeen joined Bell Telephone Laboratories Incorporated, where he carried out research on semiconductors. His work eventually led to the invention of the transistor, for which he shared the 1956 Nobel Prize with William B. Shockley and Walter Brattain. He once again shared the Nobel Prize in 1972, with Leon Cooper and J. Robert Schrieffer, for his work on superconductivity.

*Sir Frank Whittle*

May 23, 1908: Born in Wisconsin, U.S.

1936: Receives his doctorate from Princeton University

1938-45: Works at the Naval Ordnance Laboratory, Washington, D.C.

1957: Develops the theory of superconductivity

1977: Receives the Presidential Medal of Freedom, the highest honour awarded to a U.S. civilian

January 30, 1991: Dies in Boston, Massachusetts

*Willem Kolff*

February 14, 1911: Born in Leiden, Holland

1945: His device saves the life of an old woman, who then lived for another seven years

1950: Goes to the U.S., where he conducts research on artificial hearts at the Cleveland Clinic Foundation

1957: An artificial heart is implanted in an animal for the first time

1982: Supervises artificial heart implant in a human patient

## 75 Willem Kolff
[1911 - ]

Willem Kolff spent most of his childhood learning medicine from his father, Jacob Kolff. As a medical student, Willem witnessed a 22-year-old man die due to kidney failure. The incident had a deep effect on Kolff and he devoted himself to finding a solution. In mid-1940 he invented the artificial kidney dialysis machine. Today, Kolff's machine makes it possible for patients with kidney failure to live longer.

*100 GREAT*
**Inventors**

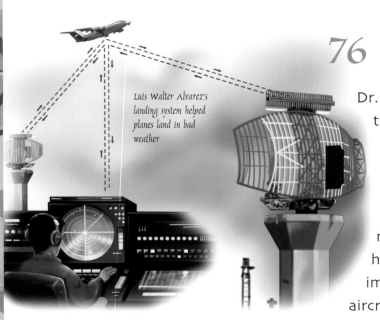

Luis Walter Alvarez's landing system helped planes land in bad weather

## 76 Luis Walter Alvarez
[1911 - 1988]

Dr. Luis Walter Alvarez held patents for more than 30 inventions and made ground-breaking discoveries in nuclear physics, but his most valuable contribution came during World War II, when he developed three vital radar systems. These were the microwave early-warning system, the Eagle high-altitude bombing system and, most importantly, a landing system that assisted aircraft to land even in bad weather. The landing system is used even today for civilian aircraft.

June 13, 1911: Born in San Francisco, California

1944-45: Involved in the Manhattan Project for the development of the atomic bomb, at the Los Alamos Laboratory; develops a detonator for setting off the plutonium bomb

August 6, 1945: Witnesses the bombing of Hiroshima, Japan

1968: Awarded the Nobel Prize in Physics for developing the hydrogen bubble chamber and using it in the discovery of unknown subatomic particles like the Y-particle

1963: Assists the Warren Commission in its investigation into President John F. Kennedy's assassination

1980: Joins his son Walter Alvarez in publishing the theory that a meteor caused the extinction of dinosaurs on Earth

September 1, 1988: Dies of cancer in Berkeley, U.S.

## 77 Ruth Handler
[1916 - 2002]

Mattel, the toy company that manufactures Barbie, originally made picture frames. One of the founders, Elliot Handler, soon started to make doll-house furniture too. After his partner, Harold Matson, left the company, Elliot and his wife Ruth took over the reins. One day while watching her daughter, Barbara, play with dolls, it struck Ruth that little girls lived their dreams through dolls. This led to her creating "Barbie", named so after her daughter's nickname.

## 78 Al Gross
[1918 - 2000]

Regarded as the founding father of wireless communication, Al Gross invented the walkie-talkie. His interest in radio communication began when he was just nine years old, when during a boat trip on Lake Erie, he first listened to a wireless. Apart from the walkie-talkie, Gross also invented the telephone pager and made important contributions to the invention of cordless and cellular telephones.

Al Gross

## 79 Gordon Gould
[1920 - unknown]

Gordon Gould did not just invent the laser, he also coined the word. A great admirer of Thomas Alva Edison, he dreamt of being an inventor as a young boy and later graduated in physics. During World War II, he worked on the Manhattan Project. According to Gould himself, the idea of laser was born one night in 1957. He defined his concept as Light Amplification by Stimulated Emission of Radiation, or LASER. However, he did not apply for a patent until 1959.

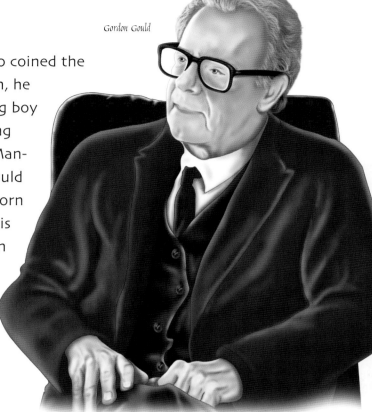

*Gordon Gould*

*Ruth Handler thought of creating the Barbie doll while watching her daughter "Barbie" play!*

July 17, 1920: Born in New York City

1977: Receives his first laser patent

November 4, 1916: Born as Ruth Mosko in Denver, Colorado, U.S.

June 26, 1938: Marries Elliot Handler

1945: Elliot enters into a partnership with Harold Matson to establish Mattel Creations (later Mattel, Inc.)

1959: Introduces "Barbie" at a toy fair in New York City

1961: Introduces "Ken", named after her son

1967: Becomes the president of Mattel

1975: Resigns from Mattel Inc.

April 27, 2002: Dies in Los Angeles, California

## 80 Charles P. Ginsburg
[c.1920 - 1992]

Known as the father of the video cassette recorder, Charles Paulson Ginsburg started his career as an engineer in a local radio station. As head of the research team at Ampex Corporation, Ginsburg developed the first videotape recorder (VTR). It marked a turning point in television broadcasting. The Ampex VRX-1000 (also Mark IV) saw the beginning of a multi-million-dollar industry. The VTR eventually led to the development of the video cassette recorder, or the VCR.

July 27, 1920: Born in San Francisco, California

1952: Joins Ampex Corporation; starts working on developing the VTR

1956: CBS becomes the first television network to use the VTR technology

1958: Granted patent for his invention

April 9, 1992: Dies in Eugene, Oregon, U.S.

1918: Born in Toronto, Canada

1934: Receives his amateur radio licence at the age of 16

1938: Invents the walkie-talkie

1949: Develops the telephone pager

December 21, 2000: Dies in Sun City, Arizona, U.S.

*100* GREAT
# Inventors

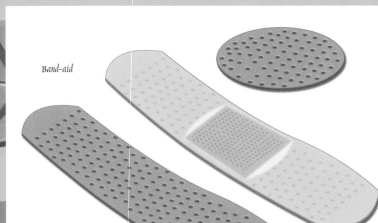

*Band-aid*

## 81 Earle Dickson
*[unknown]*

Earle Dickson invented the band-aid for his wife, who was always injuring herself while preparing food. Upon realising that the big bandages came off easily, he started to think of a better alternative. He attached square pieces of gauze to the centre of a surgical tape. He then placed crinoline to make the tape germ-free. Now, all that was required was to cut a piece of the tape to bandage the wound. Dickson presented the idea to his employers at Johnson & Johnson, who in turn sold it under the brand name Band-Aid.

1917: *Marries Josephine Francis Knight*

1920: *Invents band-aid*

1921: *Handmade band-aids are introduced to the public*

1924: *The first machine-made and sterilised band-aids are introduced*

## 82 Jerome Lemelson
*(1923 - 1997)*

One of the most prolific American inventors, it is said that Lemelson received at least one patent every month, for 40 years! In all, he owned more than 500 patents. His inventions led to the development of automatic teller machines (ATM), cordless phones, fax machines and even robotics. His innovations also led him to fight several court cases regarding patent rights. The loss of most of these cases made Lemelson determined to protect the rights of independent inventors like himself. He established the Lemelson foundation with this purpose in mind.

July 18, 1923: *Born in Staten Island, New York, U.S.*

1953: *Obtains his first patent for a toy cap*

1954: *Marries Dorothy Ginsberg*

1958: *Resigns from his job to devote himself completely to inventing*

1996: *Diagnosed with liver cancer, inspiring him to improve cancer-treatment devices*

October 1, 1997: *Dies at the age of 74*

## 83 Jack St. Clair Kilby
*[1923 - 2000]*

November 8, 1923: *Born in Jefferson City, Montreal, U.S.*

July 1958: *Starts working on the integrated circuit*

September 12, 1958: *Demonstrates his chip for the first time*

2000: *Awarded the Nobel Prize in Physics for his work on the integrated circuit*

Jack Kilby was only an average student. However, that did not stop him from inventing the integrated circuit (microchip). Kilby had just started his career with Texas Instruments, when he developed his ground-breaking device. Although it is the "planar IC" created by Robert Noyce that is widely used, Kilby is credited with starting the information age. He also invented the pocket calculator, which was the first popular device to use the integrated circuit.

*A microchip*

## 84 Rufus Stokes
[1924 - 1986]

Rufus Stokes invented the exhaust purifier (air purifier), a device that reduces the level of ashes and toxic gases emitted in smoke from factories. Stokes demonstrated that treating the smoke with his "clean air machine" made it nearly transparent, making it much less poisonous. He tested and demonstrated several models of the filters to prove that it worked. By reducing pollution, the filters helped people breathe better and also improved the health of plants and animals. It also improved the appearance and the durability of buildings, automobiles and other such objects exposed to industrial pollution for a long time.

| |
|---|
| 1924: Born in Alabama |
| January 17, 1966: Invents the exhaust purifier and files for patent |
| April 16, 1968: Obtains patent for his invention |
| 1986: Dies |

Jerome Lemelson

| |
|---|
| January 30, 1925: Born in Portland, Oregon |
| 1962: Starts work on the NLS |
| December 9, 1968: Demonstrates the NLS and the mouse in public |
| 1989: Retires and establishes the Bootstrap Institute |

## 85 Douglas Engelbart
[1925 - ]

Although Douglas Engelbart invented a number of computer-related devices, his most important contribution has been the "mouse". Engelbart's aim was always to simplify computer usage and thereby increase its popularity as an office tool. With this in mind, he developed a system called the NLS (oNLine System). Through this system he introduced the mouse, hypermedia and video teleconferencing.

The mouse is an important component of a computer today

*100* GREAT
**Inventors**

## 86 Seymour Cray
### [1925 - 1996]

An American electronics engineer, Seymour Roger Cray is best known for the supercomputers he designed. He established Cray Research Incorporated to build the world's fastest supercomputers. In 1976 he introduced his Cray-1 system, which took supercomputing to new levels. The Cray-2 followed in 1985. Cray also designed the world's first transistor-based computer called the CDC 1604.

September 28, 1925: Born in Chippewa Falls, Wisconsin, U.S.

1957: Co-founds Control Data Corporation (CDC)

1972: Establishes Cray Research Incorporated

1976: Introduces the Cray-1 supercomputer

1985: Demonstrates the Cray-2

October 5, 1996: Dies in Colorado Springs, Colorado

## 87 David Warren
### [1925 - ]

Dr. David Warren invented the flight data recorder, popularly called the "black box". While working at the Aeronautical Research Laboratories, Dr. Warren was involved in investigations into an aircraft crash. He saw that recording the conversations of the crew would provide clues to the reasons for unexplained crashes. He then invented the first "ARL Flight Memory Recorder" built to record four hours of cockpit conversations and instrument readings.

March 20, 1925: Born in Groote Eylandt, Northern Territory, Australia

1950: Becomes a rocket-fuel chemist

1953: Joins the Aeronautical Research Laboratories in Melbourne

1957-58: Builds and demonstrates the Flight Memory Recorder, but fails to arouse interest

1958: Secretary of the U.K. Air Registration Board invites Warren to demonstrate the device in Britain

1960: A mysterious crash in Australia leads to a court order making flight recorders compulsory

1962: Warren improves his original device and builds a crash- and fire-proof container for it

1967: Australia becomes the first country in the world to make flight-recording compulsory

Robert S. Ledley

## 88 Robert S. Ledley
### [1926 - ]

Robert Ledley is best known for inventing the ACTA (Automatic Computerised Transverse Axial) diagnostic X-ray scanner – the forerunner of the modern CAT scanner. Ledley's invention made a major breakthrough in diagnosing diseases and revolutionised medical research. With the whole-body scanner, it was now possible to do medical imaging and three-dimensional reconstructions of the body. Ledley was also the first to use the scanner for planning radiation therapy for cancer patients and to detect bone diseases.

June 28, 1926: Born in New York City

November 25, 1975: Granted patent for his invention

1997: Awarded the National Medal of Technology

*Seymour Cray*

## 89 James T. Russell
[1931 - ]

A music lover, Russell was often annoyed by the low quality of his phonograph records. The desire for a better recording system inspired him to invent the compact disc (CD). Russell thought of a system that would work without any contact between its parts. Familiar with digital data recording, Russell went on to apply the same principle to the compact disc that he developed. He then continued to improve his CD to include not just music, but any kind of data.

1931: Born in Bremerton, Washington

1965: Joins Battelle Memorial Institute as a senior scientist

1970: Obtains patent for the CD-ROM (compact disc read-only memory), the first of the 26 such patents in the field

*James Russel invented the compact disc with the view to improving recording quality*

## 90 Robert Dennard
[1932 - ]

*The "black box" helps determine reasons for an aircraft crash*

Robert Heath Dennard invented the one-transistor dynamic random-access memory (DRAM). Dennard's device not only increased computer memory, but also made the personal computer (PC) a reality. After receiving his PhD in electrical engineering, Dennard joined IBM's research division, working on integrated-circuit designs and memory cells. It was there that Dennard came up with his revolutionary idea of reducing RAM to a single transistor, thus also making it feasible to reduce the size of the computer.

September 5, 1932: Born in Terrell, Texas

1958: Joins the research centre at IBM

1966: Invents RAM

1968: Granted patent for his invention

1988: Awarded the National Medal of Technology

*100* GREAT
**Inventors**

## 91 Martin Cooper
### [c. 1933 - ]

Regarded as the father of mobile phones, Cooper made the first-ever call from a portable handheld cellular phone. After AT&T had introduced the first car telephone, Cooper launched his efforts to develop a "real" cellular phone. At the time, he was the general manager of Motorola's Communications Systems Division. On April 3, 1973, Cooper placed the historical call to his counterpart at AT&T Bell Labs, from the streets of New York City!

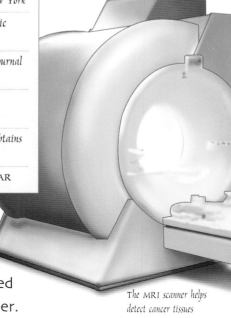

Martin Cooper

c. 1933: Born in Chicago, Illinois, U.S.

1983: Motorola introduces the Dyna-Tac model

April 1992: Establishes ArrayComm, a wireless technology company

## 92 James Fergason
### [1934 - ]

James Fergason is responsible for improving and popularising liquid crystal display (LCD) technology. The earlier LCDs used a huge amount of power and were of poor quality. Fergason changed all that with his new device. His discoveries relating to the properties of liquid crystals led to the mass production of digital watches. LCD technology is now used in calculators, computer displays and other such electronic devices. Fergason holds more than a hundred U.S. patents, most of which are for his work on LCD technology.

January 12, 1934: Born in Wakenda, Missouri, U.S.

1970: Improves the LCD and makes it commercially successful

1971: Starts manufacturing LCD at his company, International Liquid Crystal Company (ILIXCO).

## 93 Raymond V. Damadian
### [1936 - ]

March 16, 1936: Born in Forest Hills, New York

1970: Discovers the medical use of magnetic resonance

March 1971: Publishes his results in the journal Science

1974: Obtains the patent for his scanning method

1977: Builds the first MRI scanner and obtains the first image of a human body

1978: Establishes his own company, FONAR

Dr. Damadian is famous for developing magnetic resonance imaging (MRI). A talented tennis player and violinist, Damadian chose a career in medicine, showing particular interest in cancer, possibly influenced by the painful death of his grandmother due to cancer. While working at the SUNY Downstate Medical Center in Brooklyn, Damadian discovered that he could easily distinguish healthy tissues from the cancerous ones, with the help of radio signals emitted by them. He went on to construct the world's first MRI scanner.

The MRI scanner helps detect cancer tissues

## 94 Phil Knight
[1938 - ]

A sports enthusiast, Phil Knight was a middle-distance runner and trained under the famous Bill Bowerman. The competitive spirit of Bowerman had a deep influence on young Knight, who came up with an idea to end German domination of the American sports-shoes industry. Bowerman and Knight established Blue Ribbon Sports (BRS), a company that imported Japanese sports shoes and sold them in the United States. Later, the twosome took to making shoes on their own. Thus it was that BRS gave way to Nike and a new revolution in the form of sneakers began!

February 24, 1938: Born in Portland, Oregon

1962: Establishes Blue Ribbon Sports

1964: Bowerman and Knight start distributing their shoes to athletes at local meets.

1966: Opens their first retail outlet

1970: Bowerman pours liquid rubber into his wife's waffle iron, thus creating the famous waffle sole

1971: Renames the company as Nike, after the Greek goddess of victory. A graphic design student, Carolyn Davidson, creates the famous "swoosh" trademark for a fee of just 35 dollars!

1974: The Waffle Trainer featuring Bowerman's waffle sole is introduced

Phil Knight

## 95 Ray Thomlinson
[1941 - ]

Tomlinson was working on a programme called SNDMSG (short for "send message") at BBN Technologies, when he created the email. The SNDMSG programme allowed users of the same computer to leave messages for one another. He was also working on another program, CYPNET, that allowed files to be transferred between computers within the ARPANET network (later became the Internet). Tomlinson decided to combine the two to create the email!

1941: Thomlinson is born

1971: Creates the email, choosing the symbol @ to separate the name of the person and the machine in the address; sends the first message to himself, on the computer next to him. The message simply read QWERTYUIOP

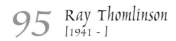

Tomlinson choose this symbol to seperate the person's name and the machine name when he created the email

## 100 GREAT
# Inventors

## 96 Nolan Bushnell
[1943 - ]

The founder of Atari, Nolan Bushnell is often referred to as the father of the video-arcade industry. Although video games were a reality even then, Bushnell is credited with turning it into a profitable industry. While still in college, Bushnell became a fan of the famous Spacewar game. Later, he created the Computer Space on the same lines. Despite its failure to arouse public interest, Bushnell went on to create the most popular game in history – the Pong. A true businessman, Bushnell had it installed in a tavern in Sunnyvale, California, thus beginning the age of video arcades.

*Nolan Bushnell*

February 5, 1943: Born in Clearfield, Utah

1970: Designs and builds the Computer Space video game

1972: Establishes Atari Corporation, a video-game company and releases Pong, the first successful video-arcade game

1976: Sells Atari to Warner Communications (now AOL Time-Warner)

1977: Establishes the famous Pizza Time Theatres restaurant chain

1978: Resigns from Atari

1984: Resigns from Pizza Time Theatres

1999: Establishes another video-game company, uWink

## 97 Erno Rubik
[1944 - ]

July 13, 1944: Born in Budapest, Hungary

1974: Invents the cube and names it Magic Cube

1975: Applies for Hungarian patent

1977: Production of the cube begins

1980: The Magic Cube is renamed Rubik's Cube after its creator

*The Rubik's cube*

The famous Rubik's Cube was the brainchild of Erno Rubik, an interior-design professor. Rubik, who had a passion for geometry, liked to teach using models made from paper, wood and cardboard. Always looking for new ways to challenge his students, Rubik thought of creating a puzzle that was simple yet required immense patience and creativity. The final inspiration came one afternoon as he watched the Danube river flow. The smooth pebbles under the water became the basis of the cube's interiors. The rounded interior made it easy to twist the cube.

## 98 Tim Berners-Lee
### [1955 - ]

Tim Berners-Lee's genius is evident from a story about his college days. It is said that he built his first computer while still a student at Queen's College at Oxford University. He made it possible with just a soldering iron, a processor and an old television. Not hard for a person who went on to create the World Wide Web (www), an effective way of distributing information globally. Berners-Lee also created such well-known web concepts as http://, HTML and URL.

*Tim Berners-Lee*

> June 8, 1955: Born in London
>
> 1989: Presents the concept of World Wide Web to his employers at CERN
>
> 1990: Puts the first website, info.cern.ch, online
>
> 1991: Makes the World Wide Web available on the Internet
>
> 1994: Establishes the World Wide Web Consortium (W3C) for the development of the web

## 99 Robert Patch
### [1957 - ]

While most inventors show early signs of genius, they usually make a name for themselves much later in life. Not so in the case of Robert Patch. A child genius beyond doubt, Patch was granted a patent for his toy truck when he was only six years old! His truck could be easily assembled and disassembled by a child. It could also be changed from a closed-van style truck to an open pick-up type.

> 1957: Robert Patch is born
>
> June 4, 1963: Granted patent for his toy truck

## 100 Don Wetzel
### [unknown]

> 1968: The idea of an ATM is born
>
> 1969: Develops the first ATM and ATM card with magnetic strip; Chemical Bank installs the first-ever ATM at its Rockville branch

Don Wetzel invented one of the most widely used machines of all time — the automatic teller machine, popularly called ATM. Wetzel got the idea when he was waiting in a line at a bank. At the time, he was working with a company that developed automatic baggage-handling equipments. He got two of his colleagues interested in the concept and together they developed the ATM and the first ATM card. Wetzel's ATM, however, did only basic functions like giving out cash. Today an ATM can perform a range of tasks, including help you deposit money *in* the bank!

*Don Wetze invented the ATM that simplified banking*

# Glossary

**Alternating current:** An electric current that changes its direction of flow at regular intervals

**Atmospheric pressure:** Pressure caused by the weight of the gases around the earth

**Ballistite:** A smokeless powder containing equal amounts of nitro-glycerine and nitrocellulose

**Barometer:** An instrument used for measuring atmospheric pressure. It is widely used to predict the weather

**Bazooka:** A weapon that is held on the shoulders. It consists of a long metal tube for firing rockets at a short distance

**Blasting gelatine:** An explosive containing mostly nitro-glycerine and a little collodion, a solution containing alcohol usually used as an adhesive

**CAT scanner:** A machine that produces 3-D photographs of the internal body structure

**Cathode-ray tube:** A vacuum tube in which a cathode emits a beam of electrons that pass through a high voltage anode before being allowed to hit a phosphorescent screen

**Coal tar:** A thick black liquid that is used for roofing and waterproofing and also to make paints and drugs

**Cobbler:** One who makes or mends shoes

**Condenser:** An instrument used to condense air or vapour. It consists of a cylinder with a piston that sucks the air in and a valve that prevents the air from escaping

**Departed:** Dead

**Detonator:** A fuse that sets off an explosive

**Dynamo:** A device that converts mechanical energy into electrical energy (like in a bicycle); especially produces direct current

**Elasticity:** The property of an object or material which allows it to return to its original shape even after its shape has been distorted; e.g. rubber band

**Electric transformers:** A device that transfers an alternating current from one circuit to another with changes in the voltage and other electric characteristics

**Electromagnet:** A magnet consisting of a piece of iron wrapped with an electric coil. The iron acts like a magnet only when electric current is passed through it.

**Embark:** To set out on a venture or journey

**Enduring:** Lasting

**Forerunner:** Anything that comes before something similar in time

**Four-stroke:** Relating to an internal-combustion engine in which the piston moves up and down four times for every explosion causing the fuel to burn and release energy

**Graphite:** A soft steel-grey to black type of carbon that is used in lead pencils

**Graphophone:** A type of photograph

**Harpsichord:** A triangular-shaped instrument similar to the piano. However, unlike the piano the strings were plucked using keys that had quills or small thin pieces of metal or bone (like the one used to play guitar) instead of hammers

**http:** A common procedure used to request and transmit files, especially web pages, over the Internet

**Humidity:** Dampness found in air

**Hygrometer:** An instrument used to measure humidity in the atmosphere

**Hypermedia:** A computer-based information retrieval system that allows a user to access texts, audio and video images, photographs and graphics on the computer

**Incandescent:** Emitting visible lighting as a result of heating

**Induction coil:** A kind of transformer used for producing high-voltage current from a low-voltage current

**Internal-combustion engine:** Any type of engine (e.g. diesel engine) in which the fuel is burned within the engine unlike in a steam engine in which the fuel is burned in an external furnace

**Intervening:** To come or lie between two things

**Iris diaphragm:** A round device whose diameter can be changed. This is commonly used in cameras to control the amount of light that enters the lens

**Kidney dialysis machine:** A machine that helps a patient whose kidneys have failed to expel waste that is usually expelled through urine

**Liquorice:** The sweet juicy root of a Mediterranean plant used in sweets

**Magnetron:** A tube that produces microwave radiation used in radar and in microwave ovens

**MRI scanner:** A machine that uses nuclear magnetic

resonance to produce electronic images of human cells, tissues and organs

**Naphtha:** Liquid mixtures that are distilled from petroleum or coal tar and that can easily catch fire. They are used as fuels and in making various other chemicals

**Navigable:** A ship, boat or an aircraft that can be steered

**Paltry:** Insignificant, meagre or very little

**Patent:** A grant made by any government that gives the creator of an invention the right to make, use and sell the invention for a particular period of time

**Perpetual:** Lasting forever

**Phonograph:** A machine that reproduces sound. It consists of a rotating cylinder covered with tinfoil or wax and a sharp pointed instrument (like a needle) that causes dents in the cylinder as it rotates

**Photoconduction:** The change in the capacity of a substance to conduct electricity due to the absorption of electro-magnetic radiation

**Photophone:** A device that produces sound by the action of light rays

**Polymer:** A natural or artificial compound such as starch containing large molecules made up of lighter and simple molecules

**Pressure gauge:** A device used for measuring the pressure of a gas or liquid

**Prolific:** Productive or create in large numbers

**Propeller:** A device consisting of a shaft and blades placed in such a way so as to thrust air or water in the desired direction thus moving the aircraft or boat in the opposite direction

**QWERTY keyboard:** The keyboard that is popularly used in computers and typewriters called so after the first six alphabets found in the first row

**Radiation:** Energy that is given out in the form of electrically charged particles, rays or waves

**RAM:** The most common computer memory that allows programs to perform necessary operations while the computer is on

**Reaper:** A machine that is used for harvesting grains

**Rivets:** A metal pin with a head on one end that is put through holes in pieces to be joined. The end without the head is then hammered so as to form a head and lock the pieces together. These round metal pieces are very commonly found on denim pockets

**Rotary steam engine:** An engine in which the steam acts directly upon the rotating object that serves as a piston; e.g. a steam turbine

**Sapodilla tree:** A large tropical American evergreen tree that gives out sticky latex called chicle

**Seismology:** The branch of science that deals with the study of earthquakes

**Semiconductors:** Substances like silicon that can conduct electricity better than insulators but not as good as metals like copper

**Shellac:** A yellow substance given out by the lac insect. It is widely used in varnishes, inks and paints

**Shuttle:** A device used in weaving that loops two threads together

**Sturdy:** Strong or healthy

**Superconductivity:** The property in which certain metals like lead and mercury lose all electrical resistance when cooled to a temperature near absolute zero

**Tavern:** An inn for travellers

**Telegraph:** A system in which messages can be sent in the form of radio or electrical signals through wires connecting the transmission and reception stations

**Thermometer:** An instrument used to measure temperature

**Thermostat:** A device, as in a refrigerator or air conditioner, that keeps the temperature of the system constant

**Tinder:** Dry wood or any other easily combustible material used to light a fire

**Torpedoes:** A cigar-shaped bomb launched from a submarine. It explodes either on contact with the target or somewhere near it

**Universal joint:** A joint that allows parts of a machine, like a car, to move freely to a certain extent in any direction. In a car the universal joint or the u-joint helps the car to move smoothly on bumpy roads

**URL:** An Internet address

**Voltaic pile:** A device consisting of several discs of two different metals placed one on top of the other and separated by pads dipped in acid. This was used by Alessandro Volta to produce current